Marbling Fabrics
for Quilts

A Guide for Learning & Teaching

Marbling Fabrics for Quilts

for Quilts

A Guide for Learning & Teaching

By Kathy Fawcett & Carol Shoaf

American Quilter's Society
P. O. Box 3290, Paducah, KY 42002-3290

Published by the
American Quilter's Society.
P.O. Box 3290, Paducah, KY 42002-3290

**Library of Congress
Cataloging in Publication Data**

Fawcett, Kathy, 1936 -
MARBLING FABRICS FOR QUILTS: A Guide for Learning & Teaching/
text by Kathy Fawcett & Carol Shoaf.
p. cm.
Includes bibliographical references.
ISBN 0-89145-971-5: $12.95
1. Textile painting.   2. Marbling.   I. Shoaf, Carol, 1954 -
II. Title.
TT851.F39 1991   746.6--dc20   90-27249 CIP

Additional copies of this book may be ordered from: American Quilter's Society
P.O. Box 3290, Paducah, KY 42002-3290 @$12.95. Add $1.00 for postage & handling.

DEDICATION

Special thanks to the Madison Nimble Fingers.
They gave us their time, trusted our knowledge and
were willing subjects for experimentation when needed.
Without their help and encouragement, this book
would not have been possible.

TABLE OF CONTENTS

FOREWORD

During a quilting class, we ran into a mutual acquaintance who showed us scraps of fabrics she had marbled. The fabrics intrigued us. We had just finished hand dyeing fabrics and were looking for a new endeavor. We decided to research the process and try it on our own. We ordered materials, set up our workshop in Carol's kitchen and proceeded to experiment.

After a lot of trial and error, we finally felt that we knew enough about marbling to invite our local stitching group to a marbling session. Each person provided her own fabrics, be they cotton, polyester blends, silks, or anything else. By sharing the cost of our supplies, the six of us spent modest amounts. We ended up with approximately two yards of fabric per person.

Marbled fabrics at quilt shows often range in price from four to six times our cost. We found that when we were able to obtain the fabric for less money because we were marbling it ourselves, we were more comfortable trying to use it in new ways. We have included color photos of some of the projects for which we have used the fabric – and we are sure that you will discover many other uses in the course of your own experimentation!

ACKNOWLEDGMENTS

Thanks to Jim Fawcett for the photography, to Larayne Cunningham for helping to make the instructions clear and to Barbara Black, Martha Bjick, Paula Newquist and Nancy Pearson for the use of their fabrics and samples to help illustrate our book.

Thanks to Valerie Crook for encouraging us to write the book in the first place.

A special thanks to Anita McCabe, a student who went far beyond what we taught and created new techniques and designs.

Photo of the Nancy Pearson block courtesy of *Quilter's Newsletter Magazine.*

INTRODUCTION

Marbling is an ancient art that involves floating paint on a liquid surface. A design is created within the paints and then printed on another surface. Traditionally that surface was paper. Bookbinders marbled the edges of the pages in many books and marbled papers were typically used as end papers for books. Traditional methods and tools for the marbling process are still in use today.

When we mention marbling to someone, we find that people know exactly what we are talking about when we refer to the marbled pattern on a certain tissue box! Paper, lamp shades, sneakers, and a myriad of other objects can be marbled. In this book we focus on marbling fabric.

We changed and refined the basic process to suit out needs, as well as our pocketbooks. Acrylic paints were substituted for the water-based paints usually contained in marbling kits.

Poor results in the beginning didn't discourage us. They instead made us even more determined to master the technique. As our experience grew, requests for classes started coming our way, and at that point we really felt that we had earned our expert label. We hope that this book of instructions will save you from repeating some of the errors we made while learning the process.

It has been a joy to see the fabrics our students have marbled and to see them used in many projects. We have gleaned a measure of new knowledge from watching our students stir and coax paints into designs unique to them.

Since marbling patterns cannot be exactly duplicated from piece to piece, the results are truly unique. One can only approximate a previous design.

Our book is the result of our experiences, both as teachers and students. We are continually learning and hope the instructions answer your questions and guide you to new quilting possibilities.

GETTING STARTED – SPACE AND SUPPLIES

Before you actually begin marbling fabrics, you will want to select the best space available and purchase or construct the supplies and tools needed.

Fabrics can be marbled indoors or out. We have, for example, marbled 1½ yard lengths in a garage and then rinsed them with a garden hose on the lawn. But, primarily, we have marbled in Carol's kitchen.

You will need access to a sink when you marble fabrics, but the sink doesn't have to be in the same room. You will also want a sturdy table to hold your marbling container. If you are working with a group, you may want two containers to marble in, which may mean you will need a fairly large table.

The size of the fabric pieces you plan to marble and number of people you plan to work with will determine to some extent the space you choose to use. You may need to limit the size of the fabric pieces you use and the number of people with whom you work if very limited space is available!

Though with care any room can be used, marbling does involve some fairly messy ingredients, so if you plan to work inside, you may want to select a room with a floor which would not be easily damaged by spills.

You can make many of the supplies and tools needed for marbling; some you may already have at home. Others you will need to purchase from one of the companies which specialize in supplies for dyeing. A number of mail order sources we have used are listed on pages 62 and 63.

These companies often offer marbling kits which contain small quantities of each of the paints and chemicals needed. If you wish, you can purchase one of these kits. For a little more money you can order individually the supplies needed. We chose to do the latter. We split the cost among six members of our stitching group, and with the supplies we received we were able to enjoy several marbling sessions.

On page 12 is a list of the various supplies you will need, followed by specific information about each of the items.

SUPPLIES

- Container or box to hold carrageenan solution (3.5 mil plastic, 2 x 4 lumber and nails if you plan to construct a box)
- Fabric
- Water softener crystals (if your water is not soft)
- Alum (aluminum sulfate)
- Carrageenan
- Pint-size jars with lids, approximately one dozen (or one for each color of paint you mix)
- Eyedroppers (one for each color of paint)
- Acrylic silk screening paints: red, blue and yellow (Optional: black, white, dark blue, brown, colorless)
- Drainboard
- Newspapers
- Trash can with plastic liner
- Paper towels
- Tools for making designs
    - hair pick
    - bamboo skewers
    - floral card holder
- Materials for making additional tools
    - 6" rulers
    - toothpicks
    - ¾"-wide packing or filament tape
    - nails
    - cardboard
    - broom straw or whiskbroom

CONTAINER: A container to hold the carrageenan solution can be purchased or constructed. The container should be 2" to 4" in depth. The fabric needs to be approximately 1" to 1½" smaller than the container. Bus trays, large casseroles or roasting pans can be used when you are marbling by yourself.

If these containers are too small or you want to marble fabrics of a specific size, you can construct a bottomless frame using eight nails and four lengths of 2 x 4 lumber. We have used a 24" x 24" frame and a 48" x 56" frame. To construct a 24" frame, cut two 28" long and two 24" long pieces of 2 x 4 lumber. Assemble a 4" deep box and drive several nails through each joint, as shown right. A con-

nails

tainer this size is ideal for marbling fat quarters and 22" x 22" scarves.

If you will be cutting the fabric into smaller pieces anyway to use it, marble enough fat quarters in the same color combination to approximate the total yardage you will need. The pieces will each be a little different, but will blend together quite well. If larger full pieces of fabric are needed, you will have to construct a box to accommodate them.

If you construct a frame, you will need to make a plastic liner for it. DO NOT use plastic garbage bags, as they are too flimsy. Hardware stores sell 3.0 to 4.0 mil landscape plastic which works well. It is available in both clear and black. It is best to set your frame up on a light surface or lay white paper on the table and use the clear plastic so that as much light as possible is reflected back up through the carrageenan, allowing you to clearly see the paint design. Cut a length of plastic so it will fit across the top of the frame and down the sides, with at least a few extra inches to spare on each side.

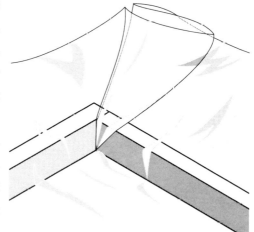

Next lay the plastic over the frame and then work it down into the frame so that it rests on the surface beneath. Be sure to carefully pleat each corner (as shown right) so that it is square all the way to the bottom.

If the corners aren't square and your fabric is tight fitting in the frame, the outer edges of the fabric will not be marbled.

It is not necessary to attach the plastic liner to the wood. The weight of the carrageenan will hold it in place. The wood frame is reusable, but you will probably want to discard the plastic liner when you are finished.

WATER SOFTENER: You will need to make the alum and carrageenan solutions with soft water. If your water isn't soft, you'll need to add water softener crystals. These come in one-pound size containers which will last quite a while. You'll only need to add one tablespoon of water softener per gallon of water. Dissolve the softener crystals in the water before adding alum or carrageenan.

ALUM: Alum allows the paint to adhere to the fabric during the marbling process. You will need to order this alum from a supplier of dyeing and marbling supplies. One pound contains approximately 2 cups; you will use ¾ cups per gallon of water to prepare a solution for saturating fabrics. DON'T use pickling alum found in grocery stores. The correct aluminum sulfate can be purchased through stores or companies selling supplies for dyeing (see page 62).

CARRAGEENAN: Carrageenan moss mixed with water is used to create a surface for floating the paints used for marbling. It comes in powdered form and can be purchased from the suppliers listed on page 62. When carrageenan is mixed with water, the resulting solution is thick, slimy and gelatinous.

JARS & EYEDROPPERS: Pint-size canning jars work well for mixing and storing paints. When marbling, keep the lids next to the jar. Lay the eyedropper inside the jar lid to prevent dipping the dropper into the wrong color paint. Eyedroppers can be purchased in pharmacies or the pharmacy section of department stores.

PAINTS: Acrylic silk screening paints (inks) are the most economical to use. We used DEKA® Print silk screening paints (inks) and Sennelier's Texticolor Iridescent paints. Make certain the acrylic paints are water-based, not Plastisol-based paints.

DRAINBOARD: A drainboard is needed to transfer the fabric from the marbling frame to the sink for washing. This can be a board of any kind or large pan. It saves the work of having to clean up drips. We used two cores from fabric bolts, taped firmly together side by side and covered with a plastic trash can liner. Be sure to cover and tape them well since the drainboard will be getting wet.

NEWSPAPERS: Save many newspapers. These will be used for cleaning the carrageenan surface and blotting the fabric. For convenience, unfold the papers and stack them flat. Two Sunday newspapers per person should be sufficient for a marbling session.

PAPER TOWELS: It is handy to have a roll of paper towels close at hand. Marbling is messy and you will need plenty of paper towels for mopping up drips and wiping your hands!

TRASH CAN: Keep a large trash can with a plastic liner in place, close at hand to take care of the gooey newspapers.

TOOLS FOR MAKING DESIGNS: Tools are used to coax the paints into the patterns that are then printed on fabric. Some of the items listed under tools in the supply list will be used by themselves; others will be combined to make tools.

Collect all of the items and then assemble the tools, following the direction provided in Section Two.

Section Two

ASSEMBLING TOOLS FOR MAKING DESIGNS

You will need to collect and construct tools for creating patterns in the paint. Many very effective designs can be made using items readily available or easily constructed. The following are some tools we use:

LARGE COMB: A tool used the most at the beginning of the paint designing process. We use a 6" plastic ruler with toothpicks taped at 1" intervals. Use filament or packing tape to hold the toothpicks to the ruler. Make certain the toothpicks are even at the tips. This tool is used in a combing motion to swirl and intertwine the paints.

BOUQUET COMB: A comb constructed using a 2" x 8" piece of cardboard. Push nail heads through the cardboard in 1" intervals, ½" from one edge. Keep the nails in a straight row. Stagger the next row ½" from the opposite edge. This tool is needed to comb the Bouquet patterns shown on pages 32 and 33.

HAIR PICK: A hair comb with teeth approximately ¼" apart. This makes a smaller version of the design made by the large comb.

BAMBOO SKEWERS: One or two are sufficient. They can be purchased in grocery stores or the housewares section of department stores.

MINI-BROOMS: (optional) Cut straw off a whiskbroom, near the stitching. Clump the pieces in dime-size bundles. Make sure the bottom edges are even and tape the top to make "mini-brooms." You'll need one "mini-broom" for each paint color.

FLORAL CARD HOLDER: One of the members of our stitching group brought in one  of the plastic holders that florists insert in pots and bouquets to hold gift cards. She used the three narrow points to make some interesting designs.

Anything which has prongs can be used to create designs in the paint. Let your imagination run free!

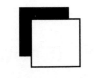

Section Three

SELECTING FABRIC

Marbling can be done on all types of fabric. You will want to select fabrics which are appropriate for their intended use in projects, but you will also want to consider the effects the fiber content and color of the fabrics being marbled will have on the design. Experiment with various fabrics to discover the way colors and designs print on each.

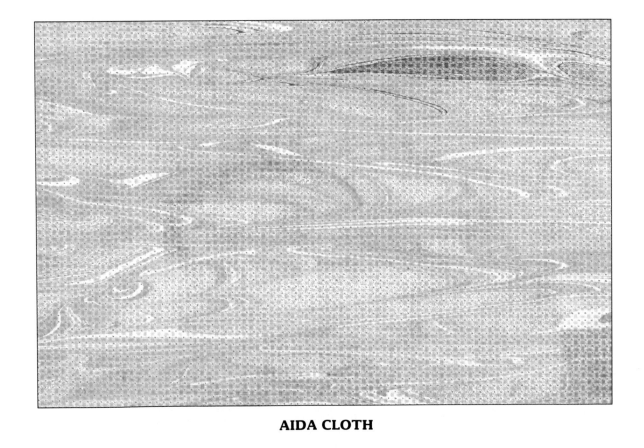

AIDA CLOTH

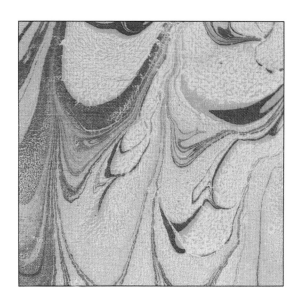

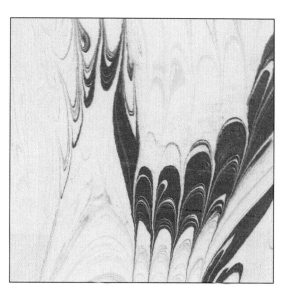

MUSLIN

BROADCLOTH

Bleached and unbleached muslin work very well for most quilting projects, but polyester/cotton blended broadcloth and other poly/cotton blends produce finer clarity. Silk produces the best results in clarity and color definition.

SILK

RAW SILK

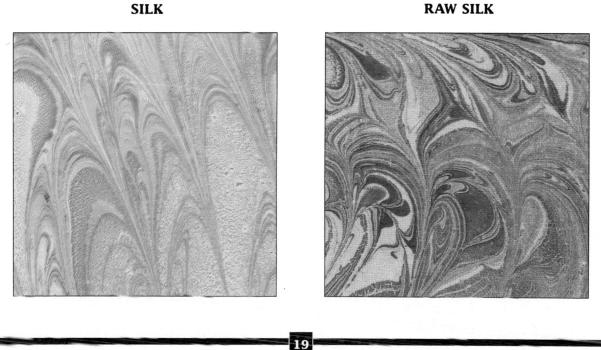

PASTEL   **NATURAL**

Often you will want to work with white or natural colored fabrics, but try pastel broadcloth or 100% cotton solids. The finished product will have softer colorations than when white or natural colored fabrics are used. Dark colored fabric often doesn't show the design very well, but can be used for special effects.

DARK

You may want to experiment with different light and dark fabrics to see what appeals to you.

Prewash fabrics as normal. If you are marbling by yourself, cut fabrics no larger than 9" x 16". Two people are needed to handle larger size fabrics.

PREPARING THE FABRIC

At least a day before marbling, but no more than a week before, prepare your fabric. Cut the fabric to a size suitable for your container. In a large bowl or bucket, mix an alum solution consisting of ¾ cup of alum dissolved in 1 gallon of softened water. Saturate your fabric in this solution. Wring out the excess solution, hang the fabric pieces and allow them to drip dry. Keep the pieces taut on the top. Hanging the fabric by one corner or bunching it causes the alum to streak. Unfortunately, the streaks won't show up until after the fabric is marbled. The paints will have different color intensities along the streaks.

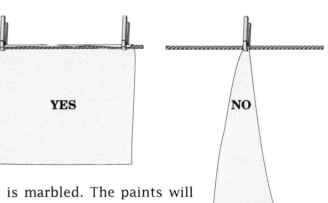

After the fabrics have dried, iron them smooth and then store them flat. Don't worry about the crinkles still in the fabric. The crinkles will disappear after the fabric is marbled, washed and ironed.

A word of CAUTION: Don't get prepared fabric wet or handle it with wet hands. Wet spots won't pick up the marbled design. If you don't marble all of the fabric you have prepared, wash the alum out of the fabric you will not be using and store it, to be prepared again when you next plan to marble. If alum is left on the fabric for a period of time, it can cause the textile to rot.

Alum can be stored indefinitely in a covered container such as a milk jug. If mold forms on the surface, strain or sieve the mixture and then reuse it.

MIXING THE CARRAGEENAN

Ordinary kitchen appliances can easily be used for mixing and measuring. First, dissolve one tablespoon of water softener per gallon of water. Pour four cups (1 quart) of softened water into a blender. Turn the blender on to its lowest setting. Take the top knob off the blender lid and slowly sprinkle two teaspoons of carrageenan into the water. Replace the knob and run the blender at its highest speed for a few seconds.

Pour the mixed carrageenan solution into your marbling box. Continue mixing carrageenan solution and adding it until the solution is about 1" deep in the container. If you plan on marbling 40 or more pieces, we suggest mixing and adding carrageenan solution until it is approximately 2" deep. If the carrageenan solution is too shallow, you will find yourself continually raking the plastic on the bottom.

You can mix the carrageenan solution just prior to the marbling session if you are using a blender and you mix the powdered carrageenan carefully, adding it very gradually. If a blender isn't available, use a hand mixer or egg beater and mix as best you can. If you are not using a blender, you will need to mix the solution approximately 12 hours prior to the marbling session. That will give any lumps in the carrageenan mixture time to dissolve. Do not worry about any bubbles or foam that accumulate.

Prior to the marbling session, lay a single open sheet of newspaper on the surface of the carrageenan. If the container is larger than the newspaper, lap papers to cover the entire surface. Make certain your trash can (with a liner) is nearby. Pick up the newspapers by quickly pulling them across, skimming the surface in one motion. Do not wait for the carrageenan to stop dripping off the newspapers. Discard them immediately in your trash can. You have just cleaned off the dust and bubbles! The solution's surface should be clean and smooth.

This solution is good for up to two weeks and may be reused. Carrageenan is a moss, an organic substance, and will rot after a couple weeks. Be sure to cover it, and do not store it in temperatures below 55 degrees or the marbling process will not work. When you are ready to reuse it, you will need to skim the surface again to clean away dust and other impurities.

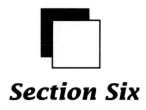

Section Six

SELECTING AND PREPARING THE PAINTS

You'll need the three primary colors: red, blue and yellow. All other colors can be mixed using a combination of these with black added for a muddy effect and white for pastels. We primarily used silk screening paints because they cost less. (These are actually silk screening inks, but we refer to these as paints in this text because rather than printing with them we use them as paint.) **Table I** shows the paints we purchased.

Silk screening paints are acrylic. Not all brands of screening paints will work. Paints obtained from a silk screening business didn't work because they contained a plastic. Check with your supplier to make certain there is no plastic in the paints you plan to use.

Textile paints are the most widely used paints for marbling. Sennelier's Texticolor and Iridescent paints are textile paints. Other brands are available. This book reflects our experiences with DEKA® Print silk screening and Sennelier's Iridescent textile paints.

TABLE I

DEKA® Print Silk Screening Paint (Ink)	**Sennelier's Texticolor Iridescent**
(8 ounces)	**Fabric Paint**
(Primary Colors)	*(8.4 ounces)*
602 Golden Yellow	055 Silver/White
605 Light Red	060 Black
609 Light Blue	
(Additional Colors)	
601 Lemon	
611 Dark Blue	
615 Brown	
600 Colorless	

Sennelier's Texticolor Iridescent paint blends with the flat silk screening paints. White by itself yields poor results and is not very stable. When blended with the flat silk screening paints, the iridescent qualities are taken on by the resulting color. The two paints do not separate once blended. Sennelier iridescent black paint is stable. While not a true black, it is dark charcoal and produces pleasing highlights.

Dark blue also highlights the other colors well. While the three primary colors yield a wide palette of colors, black and white extend that palette even further.

Colorless paint is useful when making the pebble and cabbage rose designs (see Section Eight). Colorless is just that, void of any color. When laid on the carrageenan first, it acts as any other color and keeps the next color from dispersing as much. Consecutive colors will be more concentrated and veins will occur naturally.

To start, you'll need small jars to dilute each color. Silk screening paints are extremely thick and globby. Pick a color and put ¼ of it into a jar. Slowly add an equal amount of tap water. Put the lid on the jar and shake vigorously. The paint should be the consistency of whole milk. Add more water or paint, if needed. Using an eyedropper, drop several drops onto the carrageenan's surface. If the drops stay thick and look like "BB" pellets, the paint is still too thick. Add more water and re-test. The paint drops should act like oil slicks. They should immediately start to disperse across the surface until they touch the sides of the marbling box or more paint.

After thinning the paints, you can mix paints to obtain other colors. Traditionally, a painter starts with one main color on his palette, and then blends a second color into it until the desired color is achieved. The marbling artist mixes paints in a similar way, but in jars instead of on a palette.

You can use **Table II** as a guide. The BASE color is the color you start with and the ADD color is the color you gradually add. If you want precise colors each time, use measuring spoons and keep accurate records of your measurements. We have yet to find an instance where such careful measuring was necessary.

For each new color you mix, begin with a clean jar. Put the base color in the jar, and then slowly add the second color into the base color. Stir or shake, thoroughly mixing colors until the desired color is obtained. Remember that colors will be much darker in the jar than they will appear on fabric. For example, peach will be a medium-light rust color in the jar. If you plan to mix many colors, mix them in small quantities. If you prefer not to mix the paints, pre-mixed colors are available.

TABLE II

COLOR	BASE	ADD
Plum	Red	Blue
Purple	Blue	Red
Green	Blue	Yellow
Mint Green*	White	Green
Teal Green	Green	Blue
Lt. Olive	Green	Yellow
Bronze*	Yellow	Black
Orange	Yellow	Red
Electric Blue*	White	Red blue
Pink*	White	Red
Lavender*	White	Purple
Burgundy*	Red	Black
Steel Blue*	Blue	Black
Forest Green*	Green	Black
Orange/Yellow	Yellow	Red
Nutmeg	Brown	Orange
Rust	Orange	Brown

(*indicates metallic shades)

The undiluted paints can be stored indefinitely. Diluted paints can be stored for several months. If some of the liquid evaporates, add more water. Should diluted paints become thick and stringy, discard them. Storage jars and lids should be cleaned out periodically. If the diluted paint is still usable, pour into a clean jar. Wash the dried paint out of the old jar and lids.

LAYING THE PAINTS

We suggest using small pieces (6" squares) of fabric and swirling the paints with various tools to create designs until you become comfortable with the paints, the tools and the marbling process.

Because the paint disperses or spreads on the surface, using small amounts of paint produces pale colors. Laying a lot of one color produces intense colors. Remember that, as mentioned earlier, the color of the paint in the jar will not be the color reproduced on the fabric. This change in color results from changes in the concentration of the paint.

Shake the paints before using them and several times during the marbling session. Keep the paint jars with their lids and eyedroppers together on two or three sides of the marbling box. One side should be free for the marbling tools.

Using an eyedropper, lay the paint in lines (streams) or in randomly scattered dots, covering the surface. Try to keep the dropper within an inch or two of the surface. Keep the dropper at an angle and don't shoot the paint. That will drive paint under the surface of the carrageenan, and only the paint on the surface will produce a design. Any paint under the surface will not resurface and is wasted.

Remember to be speedy, because the paint will immediately start covering the surface. DO NOT DIP THE EYEDROPPER INTO THE CARRAGEENAN SOLUTION. If you do, *wash it out* or substitute another dropper so you don't contaminate the paints with the carrageenan.

Don't try to squeeze all the paint out of the eyedropper because that creates bubbles on the surface. If you choose to print the design, any bubbles left on the surface will leave circles on the fabric. However, you may want to leave some bubbles to add interest and vary the design. You don't have to pop every bubble! To get rid of them, simply touch them with something dry, for example, a toothpick, your finger, etc. It takes something dry to break the adhesion of the bubble. (Bubbles *can* make interesting patterns. See Section Nine.)

Use two or more colors for more effective designs. You can use as many colors as you wish in any design. Once you lay the first color, lay the second color across, on top of, or around the first. The second color will disperse, pushing against the first, making the first more concentrated and therefore darker.

If there are paints around the edge of the container (from the previous fabric), you can either leave them there or comb them in after you have added paints. Incorporating them into your design can be very desirable. They are intense in color and can act as highlights. You can clean the surface if you don't want the highlights. Simply crumple several paper towels or a piece of newspaper and blot the areas involved.

Designs to be printed should have paints that are intertwined, so be sure to lay some of each color on every area of the surface. You don't want one side to be one color and the other side to be another; the design will look blotchy.

If you want highlights other than these made with paint from the edges, sparingly sprinkle dots of the paint you want to use before you add other paints. As other colors are added, the first color laid in the tray will concentrate into vivid color bands. This technique is especially useful when longer lengths of fabric, i.e. one and one half yard lengths, are marbled. In this instance the paints from the edges aren't plentiful enough to add highlights to such a large piece of fabric.

Double loading paint is a technique we use to create shades of one color. Lay the paints on the carrageenan and comb. Decide the color you want in two shades, lay more of that color on the surface and re-comb.

You can double load to intensify colors. Lay paint on the surface, letting the colors spread. Lay additional paint on top of the previous droplets. Continue with the next color. Remember, the first color laid will be the highlights, if sprinkled randomly. In greater quantities, the first color will be more vibrant. The last color laid will be the palest, providing you don't double load it. The paints will not mix to produce another color unless you comb too vigorously, i.e., red and blue will become purple.

Once the paint is laid in the box, you can begin to create patterns by combing with the ruler, hair pick, bamboo skewer, and other tools.

CREATING DESIGNS

Before creating the design you want to print, comb just to intertwine the colors you have laid (unless you are making the Cabbage Rose, Bark or Pebble designs). Use a swirling motion or any other motion you are comfortable with. When the colors are intertwined, you are ready to create a design.

To develop your design, you can comb in a circular, straight or haphazard direction. The directions of the final combing and the tools used will determine the design. Following are some of the designs that can be created using the tools you have assembled.

Large Peacock:

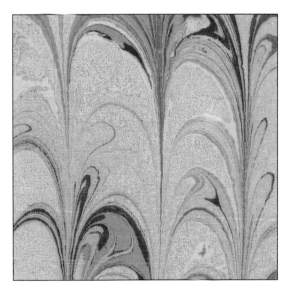

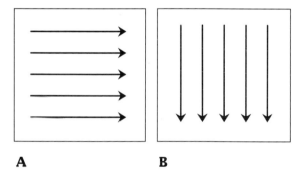

A   **B**

Using the large comb made in Section Two, comb in the direction shown in A, then in the direction shown in B. Try not to dig the ruler's edge below the surface, as this sinks the paint below the surface. Try to keep the tips of the toothpicks *just beneath* the surface of the paint.

Small Peacock:

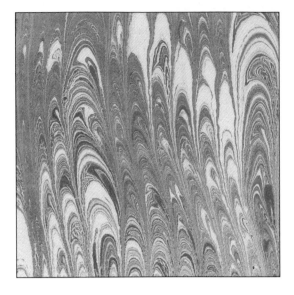

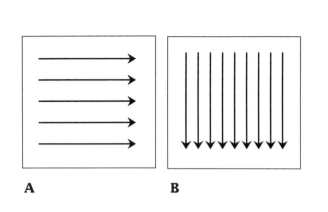

A   **B**

Use the large comb for combing the direction shown in A, but use a small hair pick when combing in the direction shown in B.

Feather:

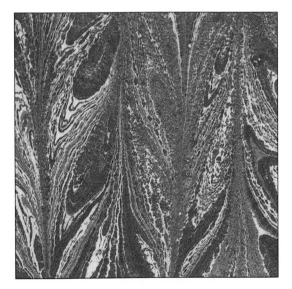

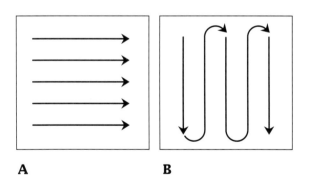

A   **B**

Comb in the direction shown in A with the large comb. Then comb with a bamboo skewer in one direction shown in B; then move over an inch or so and comb in the opposite direction as shown; repeat across the surface.

Swirls:

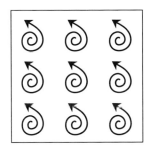

Using a bamboo skewer, make circular designs which wrap, like cinnamon rolls.

Webbing:

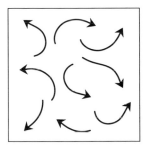

The floral pick produces designs that look like webbed feet. Pull the paints in a random fashion, using the end with three tips. Be sure to pull only the paint, not the carrageenan solution.

Pebbles:

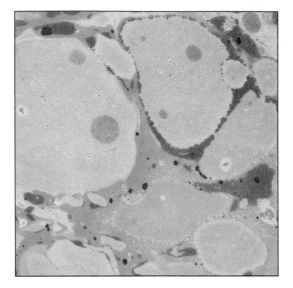

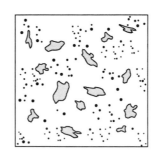

Use the mini-brooms for this pattern. Dip one into colorless paint. Tap the broom with your fingers so dots will spray out over the surface. Add the remaining colors in the same manner. DO NOT COMB.

Bouquet Pattern One:

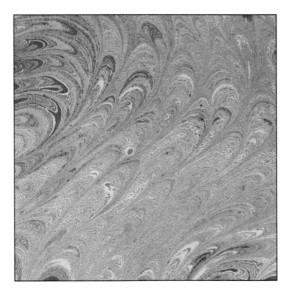

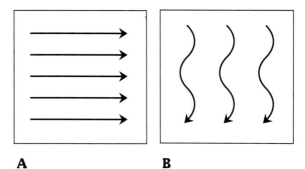

A   B

Comb first in the direction shown in A, using the small hair pick. Then comb in the direction shown in B, using the bouquet comb. When you move across the yardage to comb adjacent sections in the direction shown in B, don't overlap the combing of the last strip, but try to echo the contours of the stroke used there.

Bouquet Pattern Two:

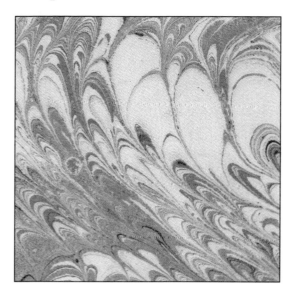

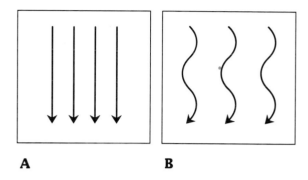

A   **B**

This pattern is very similar to the previous pattern, except upon closer inspection, you will see the colors aren't as intertwined. Comb in the direction shown in A with the small hair pick; then comb in the same direction with the bouquet comb, again echoing the contour of the initial stroke, as you progress across the yardage.

Bouquet Pattern Three:

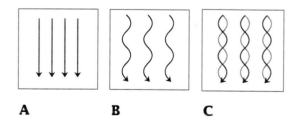

A   **B**   **C**

Comb in the direction shown in A with the large comb. Using the bouquet comb, comb in the same direction in a snaking motion, echoing the initial stroke. Still using the bouquet comb, comb again to form figure eights to complete the design.

Bark:

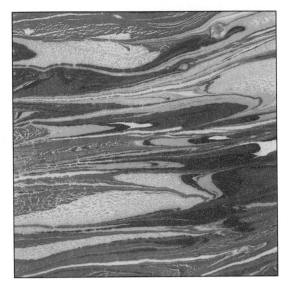

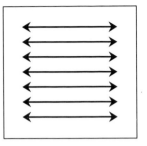

Using the large comb, comb in a left to right to left motion across the entire widths of the fabric piece. This produces a bark or water effect which is quite unlike any of the other designs.

Cabbage Rose: Developed by Anita McCabe

Cabbage roses can be made any size. The rose shown is actually about 5½" in diameter.

Using the eyedropper, randomly sprinkle colorless paint to cover the entire surface; then lay the predominant color first, in large color spots. Add the other colors on top of the predominant color. Using a bamboo skewer, comb from outside the color spot to the center, pulling colorless paints towards the center in one stroke. Repeat around the perimeter.

Random Pattern:

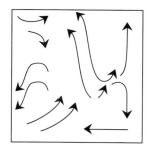

For a less rigid design, try combing in a haphazard manner. Use your imagination!

Remember, the design produced is a result of the final combing. Try other tools you might have and experiment. If you don't like the pattern, you can always re-comb it or remove it with paper and start over.

PRINTING THE DESIGNS

Once you are satisfied with your design, you are ready to capture it on fabric. Be sure there are no loose strings on the marbling side of the fabric. If left there during the printing there will be a white line where the string was. You need to lay the fabric smoothly on the surface of the carrageenan to pick up the paint. Once the fabric has touched the paint, it is permanent. Hold the fabric in a U. Slowly drop the base of the U to the surface. In a smooth movement, lay both sides down evenly. A hesitation in the movement produces a hesitation mark on the fabric.

Let the fabric lay on the surface until it looks wet. Silk fabrics look wet upon contact. Poly/cotton blends take a few moments. Muslins take the longest. Sometimes dry spots remain. Use your fingers to smooth the dry spots to the surface. They will soak up the paint. Don't worry, this will not result in a hesitation mark.

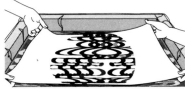

The fabric should look wet but the back side does not have to be saturated. Leaving the fabric on the surface longer does not produce a darker image. Remember, only the amount of paint in the box determines the intensity of color. We like to leave the fabric on the surface for 10 to 30 seconds before picking it up. To remove the fabric, lift it by two adjacent corners and suspend it vertically over the box for a few moments, letting excess carrageenan drip. If you don't do this, you are throwing away too much carrageenan.

The paints may start to run. Don't panic! This is excess paint. The color of the running paints will be intense, but the paint tracks will rinse off, leaving only the sharp definition of your initial design.

No matter how carefully you work, you are bound to end up with a so-called flaw on your fabric – an air bubble not popped, a string or even a hair marring the design. Although we all want perfection, these flaws can often be creatively used.

Hesitation Marks:

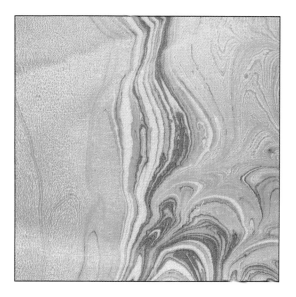

Cut into small pieces, most hesitation marks can be hidden within the design. Use the small pieces in both applique and piecing projects.

Air Bubbles:

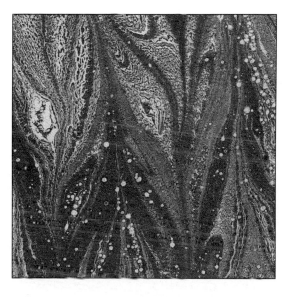

Unless pointed out, most quilters don't recognize air bubbles as flaws. A collection of small air bubbles can be quite attractive in the overall design, actually enhancing it. Larger air bubbles are a nuisance in large clusters, but randomly scattered within the marbling, the eye encompasses them within the overall design. A bubble can be an eye, a spot on a butterfly's wing ...or just a spot!

Strings:

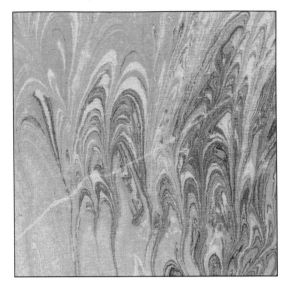

Strings are the hardest of flaws to camouflage. If the string meanders and crosses itself, you're better off cutting out the flaw and using the remainder. Strings that are linear can be cut into small pieces to disguise them. Treat hair flaws in a similar manner.

Color Bands:

These appear after marbling and occur because the fabrics were improperly dried after being treated with alum. The fabrics were folded over a line rather than being anchored to the line at the corners. The bright color band is as narrow as the line the treated fabrics were dried on. The color bands are usually next to the selvage and are cut away with it. When the color bands are well into the fabric, use them in applique where shadow effects are desired.

Paint Blotches:

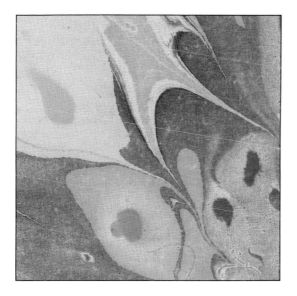

Paints that are too thick leave blotches because they can't disperse evenly. Once printed, blotches can't be corrected, but cutting them into smaller pieces makes them easier to use. Unwanted ones can be discarded.

Later on, when you are finished working and have rinsed and ironed your fabrics, you will be able to sit back and study them for a while. As you look at what you have created, look at the special qualities of your printed fabrics, caused by color laying, combing, and the "problems" just discussed. You will often find a wealth of possibilities in these unique fabrics. Keep them in mind and incorporate them creatively in future projects.

PRINTING THE DESIGNS

POLY/COTTON BROADCLOTH   RANDOM DESIGN

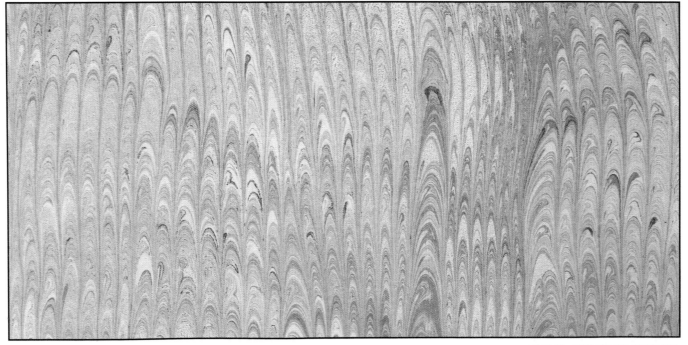

100% RAYON FAILLE   SMALL PEACOCK DESIGN

100% COTTON PIQUÉ WEAVE   LARGE PEACOCK DESIGN

LINEN/COTTON   SWIRLS DESIGN

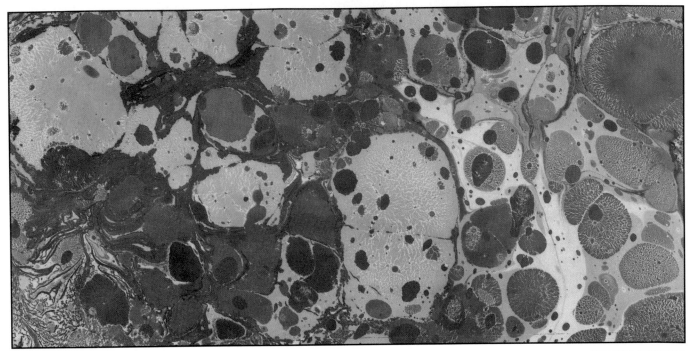

100% SILK CREPE DE CHINE   (All previous paint was removed from the tray.)   PEBBLE DESIGN

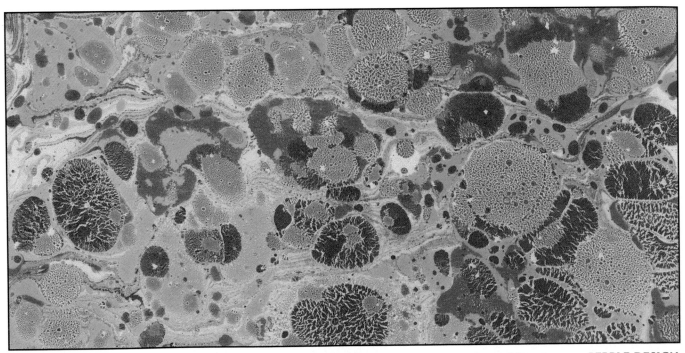

100% SILK CHARMEUSE   (The design is the same as above except the tray was not cleaned first.)   PEBBLE DESIGN

100% SILK CREPE DE CHINE – WHITE

BARK DESIGN

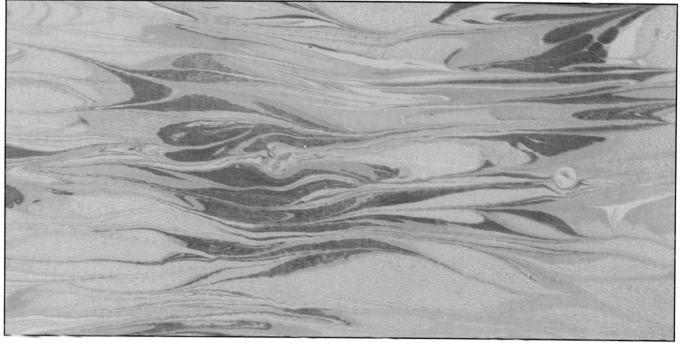

100% COTTON – PASTEL GRLEN

BARK DESIGN

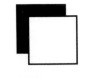

RINSING THE FABRIC

Lay the drained fabric on a drainboard and carry it to the sink for rinsing. You do not have to lay the fabric flat. A drainboard is necessary to protect floors and furniture from the dripping carrageenan. At the sink, rinse the carrageenan out of the fabric with cold water. Starting at one end of the fabric, hold a corner or edge under a slow stream, letting the water run gently until the fabric no longer feels slimy. Then move down the piece of fabric, placing the next section under the faucet. What you are doing here is rinsing the carrageenan off the fabric.

Don't rub the paint or you may also rinse paint out. The running water will work the carrageenan out. When all of the carrageenan has been removed, gently squeeze out the excess water and lay the fabric flat on newspapers. Cover with more newspaper and leave until fabric is dry.

As you proceed to marble, just build up the stack of fabrics separated by newspapers. This will absorb the water and dry the fabric. The newsprint will not transfer to the fabric. If several people are marbling with you, they can roll their stacks up to take them home. Once home, they should open up the rolls and let the fabric dry. Pieces too big for newspapers can be hung on a clothesline.

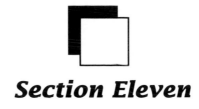

Section Eleven

CLEANING UP

Dispose of the remaining carrageenan solution by bailing it out of the marbling container and pouring it down the sink. Excess carrageenan can be stored for up to two weeks, if it is kept above 55 degrees F. Cover the tray to keep dust off the surface. The solution will clear up somewhat, becoming less murky, while still retaining a dark tint. The carrageenan's color will make seeing the paint on the surface more difficult, but it won't affect the marbling process.

If your workspace doubles as your kitchen, leaving the tray set up may be impractical. Instead, pour the carrageenan into a five-gallon covered bucket. Straining the impurities out isn't necessary. When ready to reuse the mixture, set up a tray with a new liner and pour the carrageenan into the tray. Let the solution rest for a few hours. This allows the impurities to settle, making the solution clearer.

You will probably want to throw away the plastic liner, particularly if you have been marbling for any length of time. As the carrageenan level drops, the paint dries. It often isn't worth cleaning the liner for reuse. Eyedroppers are easier to clean after soaking in dish detergent and water for about half an hour. The rubber end of the eyedropper should be rinsed out, rather than soaked, to prevent rotting.

Cleaning up is definitely quicker than setting up! After marbling for a day, you can take down the tray and clean the workspace in approximately half an hour.

Section Twelve

HEAT-SETTING THE DESIGNS

Once dry, heat-set the fabric's paint by ironing on the back side using the hottest setting specified for the fabric used. Use a hot setting for 100% cotton, medium temperature for silks. Iron each piece for a few minutes, moving back and forth across one area for about 30 seconds and then moving on to the next. If the iron base starts to get black and gummy, you have not washed out all the carrageenan. You probably should re-rinse the fabrics and dry them again. Clean the iron with a nylon or teflon scouring pad.

Once the paints have been heat-set, let the fabric rest for two weeks. After the two weeks, heat-set the fabric again and then wash it in detergent containing no bleach. This will insure that all alum is removed. Any excess alum left in the fabric can cause the fibers to rot. Silk fabrics should be hand washed in a very gentle laundry or dish detergent.

Now your fabric is ready to use.

OTHER MARBLING PROJECTS

In addition to marbling fabrics for quilt projects, there are many other applications for the marbling process.

After working and perfecting our fabric marbling technique, we decided to treat ourselves to marbled tennis shoes. They are fun and easy to do. Strangers often give us compliments when we wear them.

The shoes don't have to be new, just clean. Remove the laces and make sure the tongue is smoothed upward out of the shoe between the lace openings. Dipping a sponge into the alum solution, dab the shoes until they are saturated. Let them dry.

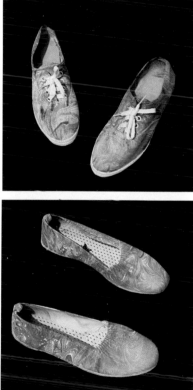

Before marbling them, stuff the toes with newspaper, keeping the tongues pulled up and smooth. If the shoes have elastic gathers across the instep, stuff the gathered area with enough papers to smooth out the gathers. Hold the shoe, top side down. Lay the side of the toe in the carrageenan and in one motion, roll the toe over to the opposite side, dipping deep into the carrageenan. This ensures that paint gets into the instep. If you miss a spot, pick an unused design area on the carrageenan and dip the unpainted area of the sneaker into the carrageenan once more. Don't be concerned if some of the painted area of the tennis shoes touches the surface. Only the dry area will pick up the design. Next hold the shoe with the toe up facing you. Starting at one seam line, roll from one side, over the heel to the other side, ending at the opposite seam line.

When the entire tennis shoe has been printed with the design, remove the newspapers which were inserted. Rinse the shoes well, especially inside the toe area. Clean up the soles, rubber edges and eyelets now. After the shoes have air dried, heat set them for 20 to 30 minutes in a hot dryer. (Make certain the shoes are totally dry when you put them in the dryer. Otherwise, the color will rub off.) After heat-setting, it is best to let marbled sneakers rest for a week before wearing them.

Any other three-dimensional object can be approached in the same manner. Once you are sure the fiber content is such that the alum solution and paint can be used, study the item to determine how to apply the paints. Look for ways of covering the entire surface of the object using the fewest number of "stops and starts," and having them fall in the least conspicuous places.

Section Fourteen

TROUBLE-SHOOTING

Problem	Cause	Solution
Paint sinks beneath carrageenan's surface	Paint isn't dilute enough.	Gradually add more water until paint disperses quickly.
Paint stays in thick rounded globules on carrageenan's surface	Paint isn't dilute enough.	Gradually add more water until paint disperses quickly.
Paint drips or runs down fabric surface once it has been lifted from carrageenan's surface	Some colors have tendency to run.	No real problem. Rinsing will remove the running paint; color will be more intense.
Paint didn't adhere to entire surface	(A) Air bubbles prevented fabric from making contact with paint. (B) Fabric had wet spots which kept the alum from doing its job.	(A) Make sure you smooth out all air bubbles with your fingers. (B) Wash & alum the fabric again to be used another time.
Colorless rings or circles on finished marbled fabric	Tiny bubbles caused by trying to get all paint out of eyedropper or stirring paints too vigorously.	Pop bubbles with dry finger or dry toothpick. Stir paints more slowly. (You may want to leave some bubbles in for texture.)
Fabric shreds with gentle pulling	(A) Alum solution was too concentrated. (B) Fabric was treated too far in advance of marbling session. (C) Fabric was too old.	(A) Adjust alum, add less to water. (B) Treat fabric only up to one week prior to marbling session. (C) Use newer fabrics.
Carrageenan solution has lumps	Dry carrageenan wasn't mixed thoroughly.	Let stand for 8 hours. Lumps should disappear.
Foam on carrageenan's surface	By-product of mixing into liquid form.	Clean surface with newspaper.
Paint sinks beneath carrageenan's surface during combing	Combs aren't being held parallel to surface. Corner of ruler is going beneath carrageenan's surface.	Slow down combing rate. Try to keep only tips of toothpicks in carrageenan solution.
You stop combing & pattern keeps moving	(A) You're combing too vigorously. (B) You're leaning on the frame or table top.	(A) Slow down combing rate. (B) DON'T lean on frame or table top.
Paint flecks appear in paints as you're using them	Paints have dried out around edges of jar.	Pour paint into new jar. Clean out old jar and lid.
Bottom of iron turns black	Carrageenan wasn't rinsed out of fabric.	Re-rinse fabrics until slick feeling is gone. Dry & heat set fabrics again.

Section Fifteen

USING MARBLED FABRICS

You may now be wondering, "How do I use the fabric I just marbled?" Most people are apprehensive about cutting up their newly created fabrics. We recommend that you start right in cutting them up. You can always marble more fabrics.

Mixing marbled fabrics and preprinted fabrics isn't difficult when you know how. The hardest step is cutting into a piece of marbled fabric. You become attached to the fabric you have created. It is pretty and you hate to cut it up. Use it anyway and get satisfaction from both making and using marbled fabrics. They look like designer fabrics, which they are, as you are the designer.

Most quilters use only small prints or solids for applique, but even with the most expert execution, these pieces can sometimes seem flat and lifeless. Contours and depth aren't conveyed to the viewer. By their very nature, marbled fabrics can add these dimensions when used creatively.

When trying to use marbled fabrics for applique, you will find that some pieces aren't suitable at all, but others may well be perfect for your needs if they are used carefully. Finding the right contours for an applique piece can be quite a challenge. There are a few guidelines that can be of help. Large pieces look better cut from an area of the marbled fabric when the marbling designs aren't very close together.

PHOTO: **Cornucopia Baltimore block, Carol Shoaf.**

If you find that the right area for the piece you need is in the center of the fabric, you must be willing to cut there. If you aren't willing to cut anywhere in the piece of fabric, use another piece. Applique is not a technique for conserving marbled fabric.

To help you isolate the contours appropriate for a particular shape, cut your templates out of see-though plastic template material. (Don't incorporate seam allowances on applique templates.) Lay the templates right side up on the right side of the fabric. Align the contours and shadings to fit the template shape. Trace around the template and cut the shape out ¼" from the traced line.

Paula Newquist used this technique to cut the bow on her floral basket shown right. She cut out the bow as one piece, finding areas of light and dark that matched the curves of the bow. Adding embroidery along the bends of the bow helped suggest the right side and wrong side of the bow.

PHOTO: ***"Ribbons and Roses" block, Paula Newquist, Madison, AL.***
(Design ©Nancy Pearson)

Using a white index card with the shape cut out, you can analyze and isolate the best areas to use more easily than you can using a clear plastic template. Don't, though, use the index card to mark the applique piece; use your template instead, positioning it on the area you located using the index card.

Marbled fabrics can be used in pieced projects as well. The Mariner's Compass block, shown at right, and the "Illusive Butterflies" and "Pin Caddy" wallhangings, page 52, are varied examples.

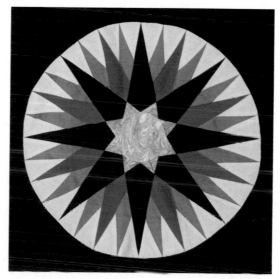

PHOTO: ***Mariner's Compass block, Paula Newquist, Madison, AL.***

PHOTOS (left to right): **_Pin Caddy wallhanging, Barbara Black, Huntsville, AL; "Illusive Butterflies" wallhanging, ©Anita McCabe, Pulaski, TN._**

Using marbled fabrics in clothing is a natural progression. Garments can be made entirely from marbled fabrics or they can contain accents of marbled fabric.

PHOTOS (left to right): **_Whole-cloth vest, Anita McCabe, Pulaski, TN; Prairie Point vest, Kathy Fawcett._**

Sometimes a particular piece of marbled fabric will even work well for an entire background. If more paint rinses out than you'd expected, leaving a pale piece of marbled fabric, that piece may be perfect for a background. Nancy Pearson took advantage of a situation like this and used the marbled fabric as the background for her applique.

PHOTO: **"Ribbons and Roses" block, ©Nancy Pearson.** *Nancy's block was commissioned by* Quilter's Newsletter Magazine, *September 1990 (No. 225) for the "Freedom Quilt" Project shown on page 40 of that issue. Photo courtesy of QNM. Photo ©1990, Jerry De Felice.*

Marbled fabric can also provide the background for quilt labels or for other needlework. Sayings stitched on marbled needlework canvas or cloth are truly unique. Simple stitching dramatically enhances the fabric design.

PHOTOS (left to right): **Saying and quilt label cross stitched on marbled AIDA cloth, Kathy Fawcett.**

If you are creating fabric specially for a project, you may find that it will require two yards of marbled fabric and you are set-up to do only fat quarters. You may find you need three yards of fabric and have only the facilities to do one yard at a time. This will not necessarily present a problem. It is possible to get the equivalent yardage without marbling it in one piece. Start with a clean tray, either by cleaning with newspapers or preferably by marbling this fabric at the beginning of the session.

Pick the colors you want in the finished project and stay with them as you marble this series. Each time you marble a piece of the fabric you want to "match," put approximately the same amount of each color into the tray. It is not necessary to count or measure.

When creating the pattern for this set of pieces, you may comb a similar pattern for each piece or make each different. If you are going to cut the fabric up for a quilt project, consistent combing patterns probably aren't important.

PHOTO: ***"Marbled Waves," Kathy Fawcett.***

If you are going to use the fabric in a project such as the blouse below, you will want more consistent combing patterns.

PHOTO: ***Kimono-style blouse, Carol Shoaf.***

You may wish to use all random combing (page 35), all feather combing (page 30) or one of the other patterns. After your fabrics are dried and ironed, spread them out on a bed or the floor and stand back a few paces. You will be surprised at how they all blend into one piece. (Use the quilter's trick of looking at them through squinted eyes.)

Often quilters try to match the colors of their fabrics exactly. We don't find that the most effective way to work with fabrics. When different colors are blended, the finished piece has movement. Subtle contrast of colors gives a sparkling effect to work. Notice the border in "Irises" doesn't match the marbled fabric triangles used to square up the center block.

PHOTO: ***"Irises" wallhanging, Carol Shoaf.***

Your eye tends to scan the fabrics used, noting the differences. The viewer's interest is held longer than if the colors matched. If colors are matched, the eye tends to meld the fabrics into one. In that case, nearly the same effect could have been achieved using only one fabric.

Marbled fabrics are a great way to create interesting quilts with exciting color and pattern combinations. By using with imagination the fabrics you have created, you can use them for just about any project, and can even use the pieces with "mistakes" or flaws. It is often surprising how well marbled farbics of all types work in various projects.

We have often been asked, "Do you discard the fabrics that you don't like?" Our answer has always been, "We never have any fabric that we dislike, just some that we like better than others," When you look at your finished fabrics, you will find that they are all beautiful – in different ways. And you will most likely find a great use for each in your future quilting projects!

Section Sixteen

TEACHING OTHERS

The transition from marbling fabrics for yourself to teaching is relatively easy once you have developed your basic skills.

As classrooms, we have used Carol's kitchen and garage, a community center and a friend's kitchen. Quilt shops, art shops, home economic classrooms or art classrooms at schools are all ideal.

Your friends and fellow guild members come immediately to mind as prospective students. Network. Let the quilt shops and other quilt guilds know what you are doing. Don't overlook sources such as adult education, continuing education, art guilds, etc.

When setting up classes, decide to marble either fat quarters or longer lengths of fabric. Offer one or the other, but never both. The frames used, the time that needs to be allotted, the paints and chemicals used and the number of students per class will differ.

A week before class, treat, iron and stack fabrics. Cut and mix paints. Prepare the carrageenan mixture the day before class or even that morning, depending on the facilities used.

Marbling fat quarters requires the help of fewer people and is less work than the longer lengths. Actual marbling time is also less.

One pound each of alum, carrageenan, and water softener, plus the primary paint colors and perhaps two extra to mix nine or ten colors total should provide enough supplies for approximately 24 students. This assumes each person will marble four fat quarters. Some paints and chemicals will be left at the end of class. (The number of students you are able to work with will depend on the number of teachers, the space, and the amount of time available. We generally work with 12-16 students, but have worked with 20 or more in a full-day workshop.

When teaching, you can let students choose their own marbling designs or you can pick four combing patterns and have students replicate them. There are advantages to each method. When allowed to choose their own combing patterns, the students will enjoy the final products more. They can marble fabrics to fill particular needs. In a recent class, one of our students wanted green fabric to look like a marble urn and another wanted fabric for pears. Both went home satisfied.

On the other hand, by duplicating combing patterns, students often gain more knowledge and understanding of the designs, developing a feel for other related designs. Students with such background are sometimes more apt to experiment on their own. Motivated students, by their own nature will experiment whether they choose their own combing patterns or follow patterns given to them.

Any size fabric pieces can be used, but larger fabrics require more time, manpower, paints and chemicals. Hence, fewer students can be included in a class. When we work with larger pieces of fabric, we have students provide their own fabric. They write their names in the selvage with a permanent fine point marker so students do indeed marble the fabric they provided. You will need to receive all fabrics a week before class. Allot enough time to treat the pieces. We charge a flat fee per piece, limiting the number of pieces to four per person. You will need to allow 15 to 20 minutes per piece in actual marbling time.

When students furnish their own fabrics, they can choose fabrics that suit their particular needs. Students we have taught have selected fabrics for use in garments and for large background areas in quilts. One student used Swiss batiste for the bodice of a dress. Another used eyelet for the collar of a blouse. Others used poly-cotton and 100% cotton broadcloth for vests. Silk jacquard and poly jacquard became blouses. Silk charmeuse and silk dobby became lingerie. We used approximately one pound of alum, one-half pound of water softener and one and three-fourths pounds of carrageenan. We pre-mixed about three-fourths of a half-pint jar of paint, per color.

When working with the larger pieces of fabric, for the marbling session we set up our frame on conference tables set side by side. You will need extra people on hand to help hold the just-marbled fabric over the frame, to let the excess carrageenan run off. This takes several minutes because of the size of the fabric used. Swiss batiste becomes very heavy, straining the arms. Raw silk or Aida cloth can tax your endurance to its limits!

Use extra people to help rinse the fabrics. We often rinse fabrics in a bathtub and hang them on a clothesline to drip a while before students transport them home. In this case, don't dry the fabrics between newspaper and roll them into a tube. Instead, gather up the wet fabrics and put them into small plastic trash bags. The students can hang the fabrics or stack them between newspapers to finish drying at home.

When the class is finished, the carrageenan level will be quite low. Since the bottom of the large frame requires large quantities of carrageenan just to cover it, the frame still holds enough carrageenan to fill a smaller frame. You can use this excess for smaller projects, providing you use it within the two-week time limit.

Another bit of information about carrageenan – we have added extra to a tray when it seemed we hadn't made enough to complete a class. Two trays can even be condensed into one, if necessary. Neither of these actions affects the marbling process.

Marbling fabrics can be taught using one of three methods. The first method involves less involvement by students in the setup preparations. The setup and fabric preparation is done prior to class. Students go home with wet marbled fabric. Heat-setting and washing fabrics are done later. This method is the most economical. Students decide if they like the process before investing in chemicals, paints and equipment. This class is taught in one session.

The second method is a variation of the first. Appointments are set up for marbling. This allows the student to come and go in a shorter time span.

A few days before class, fabrics are treated and ironed, then stored flat. Paints are cut and mixed, so they are ready to use. Three-fourths of a pint jar of each color is enough for a full-day workshop.

The third method involves less teacher preparation and maximum student involvement. The techniques are taught over several sessions. Each student purchases a complete marbling setup. All steps in the marbling process are experienced in the classroom. This "learn by doing" method helps the student develop greater understanding and self-confidence.

METHOD A
ONE-DAY WORKSHOP

Two marbling trays can be used simultaneously. Setup should be on a long table with enough space between the trays to hold the paints. Treat four fat quarters per person. All preparations should be completed prior to class. Plan on 45 minutes per student per tray of actual marbling time.

Introduction: Go over supply list. Explain construction of marbling tray, stressing size limitations if marbling alone. Discuss preparation of alum and fabric choices, carrageenan mixing, thinning and mixing paints. Demonstrate laying paints, combing, and laying fabric on carrageenan. Marble one piece of fabric and rinse, explaining pitfalls, stressing good technique. Talk about cleanup.

Work Session: Split students into three groups, rotating jobs. Have one person marble his/her fabrics, one person help lay fabrics on the carrageenan surface and a third rinse fabrics. After each student marbles his/her fabric, roll up the fabric into a tube, ready to be taken home. Make sure everyone experiences each job.

Homework: Unroll newspaper, leaving fabrics stacked. Let dry. Heat-set fabrics. Heat-set again and wash fabrics after two weeks.

METHOD B
ONE-DAY WORKSHOP BY APPOINTMENT

This is the method we use most. Many students have time constraints because of child-care duties, a job or simply a busy day. With this method a schedule of marbling times is set up in one-hour increments, with two persons scheduled per hour. We ask the students to arrive fifteen minutes early so that they can watch the previous students.

All setup preparations are identical to Method A. Use two marbling trays and two instructors. If two instructors aren't available, adjust the number of trays and adjust the schedule accordingly. Treat four fat quarters per person.

Introduction: Demonstrate laying paints and fabric on carrageenan only to the initial students. Explain equipment used, limitations that apply. Discuss fabric choices, carrageenan mixing, thinning and mixing paints and cleanup with students, just prior to actual marbling time.

Work Session: One instructor works with one student at a time. After the first fat quarter is marbled, the student will continue on, laying paints for the next fat quarter. Have another student, if one is available, rinse the fabrics. If none is available, this will be another job for the instructor. Be sure that the students get hands on experience rinsing fabrics. Stack rinsed fabrics in layers of newspapers, one stack per person. Roll into a tube after each student is finished.

Homework: Unroll newspaper, leaving fabrics stacked. Let dry. Heat-set fabrics. Heat-set again and wash after two weeks.

METHOD C
THREE-SESSION WORKSHOP

With this method, skills are taught over a three-week period, one session per week. Allow two to three hours per session.

Session I

Introduction: Provide an overview of course, explaining supplies, tools, fabric selection, types of paints.

Work Session: Fill out an order form to purchase paints, alum, carrageenan and water softener crystals. Prior to class, check with dye company to see what the surcharge for next-day or second-day delivery will be. Add this charge to the cost and collect fees for a group order.

Homework: Collect supplies for constructing marbling tray, assembling combing tools, and mixing paints and alum. Read Section One through Section Six of this book.

Session II

Introduction: Distribute the marbling supplies ordered during the last session.

Work Session: Students each complete the following activities. Construct marbling box, drainboard, combs and mini-brooms. Mix one gallon of alum solution and store in a plastic milk jug. Thin paints and mix desired colors.

Homework: Treat four fat quarters several days prior to the next session. Gather supplies for mixing carrageenan solution. Bring five gallon bucket with lid to next session. Read Section Seven through Section Twelve.

Session III

Introduction: Review combing techniques and patterns. Demonstrate laying fabric on carrageenan. Discuss rinsing and transporting wet marbled fabrics home, as well as heat-setting and laundering fabrics.

Work Session: Pair up students. While one student marbles his/her fabrics, the other assists in laying fabrics on carrageenan, lifting them, and rinsing the carrageenan out of them. When finished, students exchange roles. Leftover carrageenan is transported home in covered buckets for later use or disposal.

Homework: Heat-set fabrics once dry. Heat-set again and wash fabrics after two weeks.

SOURCES

Paints (Inks):

Dharma Trading Co.
Dept. SN, Box 916
San Rafael, CA 94915
1-800-542-5227

Rupert Gibbon & Spider, Inc.
P.O. Box 425
Healdsburg, CA 95448
1-800-442-0455

Art Supply Warehouse
360 Main Ave.
Norwalk, CT 06851
1-800-243-5038

Pearl Paint
308 Canal St.
New York, NY 10013
1-800-221-6845

All companies carry DEKA® Print Silk Screening Ink, though it may not be listed in their catalogs. You may have to ask for additional information. For other mail order sources, call Decart, (802) 888-4217. For additional sources of Texticolor products, contact Savoir Faire, P.O. Box 2021, Sausalito, CA 94966; (415)332-4660.

Chemicals:

Brooks & Flynn, Inc.
Box 2639
Rohnert Park, CA 94927-2639
(707) 584-7715

Pro Chemical & Dye, Inc.
P.O. Box 14
Somerset, MA 02726
(508) 676-3838

Dharma Trading Co.
Dept. SN, Box 916
San Rafael, CA 94915
1-800-542-5227

Rupert Gibbon & Spider, Inc.
P.O. Box 425
Healdsburg, CA 95448
1-800-442-0455

Silk Scarves and Fabrics:

Brooks & Flynn, Inc.
Box 2639
Rohnert Park, CA 94927-2639
(707) 584-7715

Exotic Silks
1-800-345-SILK
1-800-945-SILK (In California)

Thai Silks
Dept. SN
252 State St.
Los Altos, CA 94022
1-800-945-SILK
1-800-221-SILK (In California)

Dharma Trading Co.
Dept. SN, Box 916
San Rafael, CA 94915
1-800-542-5227

Rupert Gibbon & Spider, Inc.
P.O. Box 425
Healdsburg, CA 95448
1-800-442-0455

Published Patterns:

Ribbons and Roses Block (page 51, 53)
Nancy Pearson
(Send SASE)
5815 Keeney Street
Morton Grove, IL 60053

Kimono-Style Blouse (page 54)
M'Art Designs
(Send SASE)
30 S. Street Albans
St. Paul, MN 55105

Illusive Butterflies Wallhanging (page 52)
Anita McCabe
Hart House
131 S. First Street
Pulaski, TN 38478

Prairie Point Vest (page 52)
Prairie Place
10522 Black Walnut Ct.
Dallas, TX 75243

YOUR OWN RECORDS

BIBLIOGRAPHY

"Freedom Quilt Project," *Quilter's Newsletter Magazine*, September, 1990.

Grunebaum, Gabriele. *How to Marbleize Paper*, Mineola, NY, Dover Publications, 1984.

Maurer, Diane Phillippoff and Paul Maurer. *An Introduction to Carrageenan and Water Color Marbling*, 1984.

"Marbling Fabric," *Sunset*, August, 1988.

ABOUT THE AUTHORS

KATHY FAWCETT

CAROL SHOAF

Kathy and her husband are retired and live in their motorhome, traveling around the country looking for quilt shows and fishing holes. Besides quilting and sewing, she enjoys knitting and many forms of needlework. She also enjoys tying flies for their hobby of fly fishing. As a result of traveling, she has a network of quilting friends from coast to coast.

Carol and her husband are the parents of two young boys, but she always fits quilting time into her busy schedule. Besides quilting and teaching, Carol enjoys creating new fabrics and textures through the process of marbling and dyeing in order to make her work more original. Although quilting is her first love, she also enjoys traveling and cherishes friends made during her many moves.

∽ American Quilter's Society ∽

dedicated to publishing books
for today's quilters

The following AQS publications are currently available:

American Beauties: Rose & Tulip Quilts
by Gwen Marston & Joe Cunningham
#1907: AQS, 1988, 96 pages, softbound, $14.95

America's Pictorial Quilts by Caron L. Mosey
#1662: AQS, 1985, 112 pages, hardbound, $19.95

Applique Designs: My Mother Taught Me to Sew
by Faye Anderson
#2121: AQS, 1990, 80 pages, softbound, $12.95

Arkansas Quilts: Arkansas Warmth
Arkansas Quilter's Guild, Inc.
#1908: AQS, 1987, 144 pages, hardbound, $24.95

The Art of Hand Appliqué by Laura Lee Fritz
#2122: AQS, 1990, 80 pages, softbound, $14.95

...Ask Helen More About Quilting Designs by Helen Squire
#2099: AQS, 1990, 54 pages, 17x11, spiral-bound, $14.95

Collection of Favorite Quilts, A by Judy Florence
#2119 AQS, 1990, 136 pages, softbound, $18.95

Dear Helen, Can You Tell Me? ...all about quilting designs
by Helen Squire
#1820: AQS, 1987, 56 pages, 17 x 11, spiral-bound, $12.95

Dyeing & Overdyeing of Cotton Fabrics by Judy Mercer Tescher
#2030: AQS, 1990, 54 pages, softbound, $9.95

Fun & Fancy Machine Quiltmaking by Lois Smith
#1982: AQS, 1989, 144 pages, softbound, $19.95

Gallery of American Quilts: 1849-1988
#1938: AQS, 1988, 128 pages, softbound, $19.95

Gallery of American Quilts 1860-1989: Book II
#2129: AQS, 1990, 128 pages, softbound, $19.95

The Grand Finale: A Quilter's Guide to Finishing Projects
by Linda Denner
#1924: AQS, 1988, 96 pages, softbound, $14.95

Heirloom Miniatures by Tina M. Gravatt
#2097: AQS, 1990, 64 pages, softbound, $9.95

Home Study Course in Quiltmaking by Jeannie M. Spears
#2031: AQS, 1990, 240 pages, softbound, $19.95

The Ins and Outs: Perfecting the Quilting Stitch
by Patricia J. Morris
#2120: AQS, 1990, 96 pages, softbound, $9.95

**Irish Chain Quilts: A Workbook of Irish Chains & Related
Patterns** by Joyce B. Peaden
#1906: AQS, 1988, 96 pages, softbound, $14.95

Missouri Heritage Quilts by Bettina Havig
#1718: AQS, 1986, 104 pages, softbound, $14.95

Nancy Crow: Quilts and Influences by Nancy Crow
#1981: AQS, 1990, 256 pages, hardcover, $29.95

No Dragons on My Quilt by Jean Ray Laury with
Ritva Laury and Lizabeth Laury
#2153: AQS, 1990, 52 pages, hardcover, $12.95

Oklahoma Heritage Quilts
Oklahoma Quilt Heritage Project
#2032: AQS, 1990, 144 pages, softbound, $19.95

**Scarlet Ribbons: American Indian Technique for Today's
Quilters** by Helen Kelley
#1819: AQS, 1987, 104 pages, softbound, $15.95

Sets & Borders by Gwen Marston and Joe Cunningham
#1821: AQS, 1987, 104 pages, softbound, $14.95

Somewhere in Between: Quilts and Quilters of Illinois
by Rita Barrow Barber
#1790: AQS, 1986, 78 pages, softbound, $14.95

Stenciled Quilts for Christmas by Marie Monteith Sturmer
#2098: AQS, 1990, 104 pages, softbound, $14.95

Texas Quilts–Texas Treasures
Texas Heritage Quilt Society
#1760: AQS, 1986, 160 pages, hardbound, $24.95

Treasury of Quilting Designs, A by Linda Goodmon Emery
#2029: AQS, 1990, 80 pages, 14"x11", spiral-bound, $14.95

These books can be found in local bookstores and quilt shops. If you are unable
to locate a title in your area, you can order by mail from AQS, P.O. Box 3290,
Paducah, KY 42002-3290. Please add $1 for the first book and 40¢ for each
additional one to cover postage and handling.